Reading STREET

Grade 1

Scott Foresman

Readers' Theater
Anthology

PEARSON

Scott Foresman

Editorial Offices: Glenview, Illinois • Parsippany, New Jersey • New York, New York
Sales Offices: Needham, Massachusetts • Duluth, Georgia • Glenview, Illinois
Coppell, Texas • Sacramento, California • Mesa, Arizona

Acknowledgments

Poetry

P4 "Puppy" by Lee Bennett Hopkins. Copyright © 1974, 1995 by Lee Bennett Hopkins. First appeared in *Good Rhymes, Good Times*, published by HarperCollins. Reprinted by permission of Curtis Brown, Ltd.

P5 "Kittens" by Myra Cohn Livingston. Reprinted with permission of Margaret K. McElderry Books, an imprint of Simon & Schuster Children's Publishing Division from *Worlds I Know and Other Poems* by Myra Cohn Livingston. Text copyright © 1985 Myra Cohn Livingston.

P6 "Making Friends" by Eloise Greenfield, from *Nathaniel Talking* by Eloise Greenfield. Copyright © 1988 by Eloise Greenfield. Reprinted by permission of Nancy Gallt Literary Agency.

P7 "The End" by A. A. Milne, from *Now We Are Six* by A. A. Milne, illustrated by E. H. Shepard, copyright 1927 by E. P. Dutton, renewed © 1955 by A. A. Milne. Used by permission of Dutton Children's Books, A Division of Penguin Young Readers Group, A Member of Penguin Group (USA) Inc., 345 Hudson Street, New York, NY 10014. All rights reserved.

P8 "Everything Grows." Words by Raffi, D. Pike. Music by Raffi. © 1987 Homeland Publishing (CAPAC). A division of Troubadour Records Ltd. All rights reserved. Used by permission.

P9 "Honey Bear" by Elizabeth Lang.

P10 "Sunflakes" from *Country Pie* by Frank Asch, 1979, Greenwillow Books, text only.

P11 "Quack, Quack!" from *Oh Say Can You Say?* by Dr. Seuss, copyright TM and copyright © by Dr. Seuss Enterprises, L.P. 1979. Used by permission of Random House Children's Books, a division of Random House, Inc.

P12 "I Speak, I Say, I Talk" by Arnold Shapiro, © World Book, Inc. By permission of the publisher. www.worldbook.com.

ISBN: 0-328-14729-X

Copyright © Pearson Education, Inc.

Contents

Unit 1 Animals, Tame and Wild

What Will I Be? by Alisha Fran-Potter

Unit 2 Communities

Kate Goes to the Fun Fest by Susan DiLallo

Unit 3 Changes

Flowers in January by Judy Freed

Unit 4 Treasures

Show and Tell Day by Jim Hughes

Unit 5 Great Ideas

Do You Live in a Nest? by Carmen Tafolla adapted by Don Abramson

Poetry

© Pearson Education 1

Practice with a Purpose

by Sam Sebesta

As indicated in the directions in this book, Readers' Theater is a performance activity with a simple format. Costumes, makeup, and scenery are not required. Action is minimal. Because scripts are used, there's no lengthy time spent memorizing lines.

The goal is a shared oral reading performance that rocks the rafters, whether an audience is present or not. People with long memories compare it to radio drama in days of old. Yet there's nothing out-of-date about Readers' Theater. Its benefits are recognized by modern researchers. Listen to this:

ABOUT THE AUTHOR
Sam Sebesta is a Professor Emeritus from the College of Education at the University of Washington in Seattle. He continues to write and do research in children's literature, decoding in linguistic development, oral reading fluency, and reader response.

TEACHER *(puzzled):* Why are we doing Readers' Theater?

READING PROFESSOR *(reading from a scholarly paper):* "Readers' Theater promotes fluency and expression as a result of repeated reading and encouragement to make the performance sound natural and meaningful."

STUDENT 1 *(aside):* Will that be on the test?

No, that won't be on the test, although it's a good rationale for teachers to know about. Beyond this, it might be beneficial to discuss the reasons for Readers' Theater with your class.

TEACHER *(still puzzled):* Why are we doing Readers' Theater?

STUDENT 2: Because it's fun.

STUDENT 3: Because you learn to get the words right.

STUDENT 4: You learn to speak up so others can hear you.

STUDENT 5 *(the reflective one):* It's good for the imagination.

Good reasons, all. Here are five more, gleaned from comments during Readers' Theater classes and workshops:

"You get practice with a purpose."

The purpose, of course, is to present a worthy performance. The practice? It begins the moment scripts are passed out. It continues as students take their parts home or to a quiet corner to practice their lines. It flourishes in group rehearsal.

"You learn to make it sound like people talking."

A smooth delivery—flow of language, not word-by-word—is an objective in Readers' Theater that students can understand. How to achieve it? Practice reading a line and then look up and say it directly to another character. Pretty soon the fluency will come.

"More of you get to read at one time."

In this student's class, several groups are rehearsing their scripts simultaneously before they come together to perform for each other. The ratio of readers to listeners is higher than you'd find in classes where one reads and all others listen. Hence, there's more practice, more involvement.

"You learn to get into character."

Sounds too grown-up? Not at all! Children realize, from the start, that the way to portray Chicken Little is to try running like Chicken Little and talking like Chicken Little. Using mime and made-up speeches to help "get into character" may be a useful device to prepare for Readers' Theater. And there may be a more lasting payoff: readers who enjoy reading often see themselves in the roles of the characters they're reading about.

"It's reading you get to do with your friends."

Avid readers, when interviewed, speak frequently about the social value of reading, praising reading activities that have them interacting with peers. Non-avid readers who think of reading as a lonely task may also find that interactive activities such as Readers' Theater and Choral Reading alter attitudes toward the positive.

These, then, are benefits you may discover from Readers' Theater and Choral Reading. There may be more. The effects of good oral reading may be internalized, resulting in improved silent reading. Hence, speaking and listening to complex style, dialogue in character, and other features of print contribute to effective silent reading. It's no coincidence that avid readers (i.e., children and young adults who read voluntarily an hour or more a day) cite reading aloud and being read to as the major factor leading to their success.

With all these reasons in mind, Scott Foresman Reading Street offers you the directions and selections in this book. We hope you enjoy them. We want you to find them useful as a component of a powerful reading program.

Readers' Theater in Your Classroom

by Alisha Fran-Potter

Staging the Play

ACTING AREA

If you don't have a stage at your disposal, your classroom will work fine. First you need to define a functional acting area. This could be the front or back of the room with some or all of the desks pushed out of the way. It could be a taped-off area on the floor. If you need or want to leave all your desks in place, you will need enough space in front of the room for children to stand in a row. It may take some trial and error before you decide what will work best for your class and room layout. Explain to your children and train them how to prepare the acting area when you give the signal.

ABOUT THE AUTHOR

Alisha Fran-Potter is a Drama Specialist with the Glenview, Illinois, public schools. She has taught in classrooms at grades K, 1, and 2, and speech, drama, and language arts at

MOVEMENT AND BLOCKING

Traditionally, Readers' Theater is performed with the actors seated on chairs or stools in a row facing the audience, with their scripts in their hands or on stands in front of them. Actors do not memorize their parts but read them or at least refer to their scripts as they act. In this traditional method, actors do not look at each other but keep their focus out front. You can include movement in your production or not. Decide before you start how much movement there will be. Keep in mind that if children have scripts in their hands, their movements must be limited. If they remain in place, they might gesture with one free hand.

Any movement about the stage you have the actors do is called *blocking*. Your blocking choices depend on your acting area. If you have the space and want to have your actors move about freely, do so. However, if your acting area is limited, keep the blocking simple, perhaps just having the actors move from one chair to another, cross the stage, or come and go in the acting area.

If the actors are up and moving around, you need to consider their focus (whom they are talking to), and angle (the direction they face). Actors should not face each other directly, but rather turn their bodies slightly toward the audience.

If there is a place that remains the same throughout the story, such as a house or a lake, you might tape an area out on the floor or block it off with chairs or markers. This way all actors know where the place is within the acting area. You can designate entrances and exits in the same way. Primary children do well with these areas marked in tape.

ENTRANCES AND EXITS

For a smooth-running performance, go over entrances and exits before you rehearse the play.

- Actors can all enter at the same time, go to their assigned places, and then all exit at the same time. Or, they can all be "discovered" by lights up at the beginning—with lights down to signal the end.

- Actors can enter as their characters come into the story and then stay or leave and come back. You will need to decide if all the actors stay on stage after their parts are finished. (If they remain, they can all share a curtain call.)

- Actors can remain at their desks until it is their turn to perform, do their roles, and then go back to their seats. This works only if your classroom is big enough to accommodate a seating area and separate acting area.

ASSIGNING PARTS

Plan in advance how parts will be assigned and explain the process to your children. Some ways to do this are:

Volunteers This method allows children to volunteer for the parts they are interested in. Go though all the parts and describe them if necessary. Then explain that when you ask who is interested in playing each part they should raise their hands. Suggest that children have second and third choices in mind because they won't always get their first choices. If you know that a volunteer can't handle a specific part for whatever reason, choose another child and give the first child a more appropriate part. This works better with some groups than with other groups, and you must assess your children's abilities to handle volunteering.

Draw Markers To assign parts randomly, make up sticks with the children's names on them. Choose a stick and assign that person the part that is up next. This works well if all the parts are about the same in length and difficulty—and if the parts are gender-neutral. You will have to use your discretion, however, to avoid choosing a child who can't handle the reading of a role because it is large or because it will embarrass the child for some reason.

Teacher Choice Do this ahead of time to save class time. Simply go through the cast list and the class list and decide who will play what part. This works well—and indeed may be necessary—if there are varied abilities in the class and the roles vary much in length. But you must know your children and the parts in the play well in order to use this method.

SCENERY AND PROPS

Scenery provides the *setting*—where the story takes place. If you have access to a curtain backdrop, use it by all means. Chances are, however, that you are stuck with a wall of your classroom. If you have the space, you might be able to arrange desks, tables, carts, easels, chairs, and so on to suggest a setting. You might create a scene in colored chalk on your chalkboard. Keep in mind, however, that the best scenery is created in the imaginations of your audience.

Props are anything the actors handle. Traditional Readers' Theater uses no props, but if you choose to use props, keep them simple. Remember that the actors still have to manipulate their scripts. If the play calls for a bag or a purse, the actor can use a backpack or coat. Other ordinary classroom items that can serve as props include: books, clipboards, pencil cases, boxes, book ends, pens or pencils, paper, note cards, notebooks, cups, vases, water bottles. It is best to start the first couple of times without any props and then add them as you and the children grow more comfortable.

Adapting Scripts

Ideally, every child in a class or group will have his or her own role in Readers' Theater. If these scripts have too many or too few roles for your class, you may need to adapt them to fit. To reduce characters:

- Eliminate parts that are redundant or not vital to the plot. For example, reduce four narrators to two by having Narrator 1 read lines designated Narrator 1 and Narrator 3, and so on.

- Take out parts with animal sounds or cheering crowds and just let the audience infer them.

- Characters with single lines or few lines can be doubled by actors who aren't in the same scene.

- Perform only scenes for which you have enough actors. You can summarize or narrate missing scenes that are needed to get the story across.

To add characters:

- If there are many Narrator lines, divide them up to allow for more narrators.

- Have two or more students play a role at the same time. If there is a cat in the story, turn it into two cats. They can alternate lines or recite them in unison.

- Add a counterpart character and have them say their lines together or divide the lines. For example, if there is a Queen in the story, create a King.

- If many extra parts are needed, cast by scene. For example, have different actors play the King in Scene 1 and Scene 2.

- You can also put together several complete casts and perform the play several times. That way, the actors in the first performance can be the audience in subsequent performances.

Note that the suggestions for simultaneous reading also work well to help children with special needs or ELL children who are just learning English.

Adapting Trade Books for Readers' Theater

You can adapt any kind of book into a Readers' Theater script. But not every story is equally suited to the stage. Look for a story with a strong narrative line. An easy-to-follow plot adapts more effectively than a plot or story line that is too complex. If it feels complicated, you might need to simplify the plot somehow. Even nonfiction books can be turned into scripts, but among those, the books with strong narrative lines—such as biography or history—will be most effective. Here are some further elements to consider:

Narration When you are adapting your script, first eliminate all speech tags, such as "he said" and "Josefina replied." Eliminate lengthy descriptions. If you feel some description is necessary, try to put it in the mouth of a character who has a reason to describe something.

Narrators can be very useful, but try to keep their function to introducing or summarizing the story. Sometimes they may be necessary to make transitions between scenes. However, don't rely on narrators to tell the story. For example, don't write:

NARRATOR: It is early Monday morning. Mary is eagerly waiting for friends to look at her garden before the judges come. Finally Tessa arrives.

MARY: I'll show you my flowers.

NARRATOR: Together they walk to the garden in back of the house. They see beautiful bright yellow sunflowers and blazing red poppies.

Aim to show, not to tell. In other words, dramatize, don't narrate. For example, you might write:

NARRATOR: It is early Monday morning. Mary is eagerly waiting.

MARY: Good morning, Tessa!

TESSA: Hi, Mary. I've come to see that award-winning garden of yours.

MARY: I hope. But I'm glad you could come before the judges get here.

TESSA: So am I. I can't wait to see what you've done this year. I hear it's beautiful and full of color.

MARY: Oh, it is! I have bright yellow sunflowers and blazing red poppies. Here, let me show you. It's out back. Follow me.

You will find that it is helpful to have characters repeat each other's names often. This helps the audience (and the actors) keep track of who is speaking, especially when there are a lot of characters in a scene.

Dialogue Look at the dialogue in a book to see how much there is. Some dialogue you might be able to use directly in your script. Some you may need to simplify or pare down. Some dialogue you may decide to break up into smaller units, so that one character doesn't talk for too long at one time.

Be sure that the dialogue is appropriate for the age group you're working with. If not, you may be able to make it more appropriate by cutting or substituting some words or phrases.

Repetition Repetition may be of actions or of language. Repetition of actions allows actors—and the audience—to follow the story line more easily. For example, the First Pig builds a house of straw, the Second Pig builds a house of twigs, and the Third Pig builds a house of bricks.

Repetition of language might be a repeated phrase or sentence such as the Wolf's line, "I'll huff and I'll puff and I'll blow your house down!" which he says before his attack on each Pig's house.

Younger children especially do well with repetition. But many folk tales appropriate to higher levels develop their plot lines through the use of repetition.

Group Characters These allow for multiple roles. For example, if you have twenty-six actors with one main character and five supporting characters, all can have a role. One or two actors can play the main character, and then several actors can play each of the supporting characters. For example, take the story *Anansi and the Moss-Covered Rock* by Eric Kimmel.

Anansi, the spider, is walking though the forest when he finds a magic rock. He uses this rock to trick his friends so he can take their food. Little Bush Deer won't let Anansi fool him, though, and teaches Anansi a lesson in turn.

One or two actors can play Anansi, one or two can play the rock, and the rest of the actors can be divided among the other animals. So you might have two or three Lions, Elephants, Rhinoceroses, Hippopotamuses, Giraffes, Zebras, and Little Bush Deers.

Special Effects

You can create effective Readers' Theater using nothing but the actors' voices. However, if you want to add to the theatrical experience, consider the following:

MUSIC

You can use recorded or live music (such as a piano or guitar) to make transitions between scenes, to show the passage of time, or for background to heighten the mood. For example, in "Kate Goes to the Fun Fest," you can add music to the hippo ride to make it sound like a carousel. You could use a triangle, tambourine, xylophone, music box, or musical recording to accent the magical appearance of flowers and grapes in "Flowers in January." If you are using recorded music, practice cueing it up during rehearsals.

LIGHTING

If you are working on a stage with a lighting system, you can either open the curtain or bring the lights up on your actors already in place. If the actors must take their places in view of the audience, you can dim the lights to black and then bring them up to signal the start of the performance.

About These Scripts

Potential for Accuracy This is a rating given to reading materials to measure how well children can be expected to read the materials successfully. The rating is based on three factors:

- **Decodable words** They follow the rules of phonics that children are learning in grade 1.
- **High-frequency words** They are taught early because people use them every day.
- **Story words** They appear in the stories that children are hearing and reading in grade 1. They are taught in the context of the stories.

The scripts in this anthology are meant to accompany readers and teaching materials in Scott Foresman's Reading Street, grade 1. They were carefully prepared, taking into account the unit themes and the three factors listed above. If the scripts are used after the stories are taught in consecutive order in each unit, the scripts should achieve a 95% or better potential for accuracy.

About the Playwrights

Alisha Fran-Potter is a Drama Specialist with Glenview (IL) School District 34. She has her BS in Education and her Masters in Curriculum and Instruction, with an emphasis in Fine Arts. She has taught Kindergarten, 1st and 2nd grade, Drama for K-8, and 6-7-8-grade Drama and Speech. Mrs. Fran-Potter developed, wrote, and implemented fine arts curriculums for Districts 34 and 81. She has presented at the Illinois Reading Council and taught for Glenview University.

Susan DiLallo wrote a humor column for the Rye, New York *Record*. She won the Kleban and the Richard Rodgers Awards to develop her musical *Once Upon a Time in New Jersey,* which was workshopped and produced in Allentown, Pennsylvania. She also won the Hangar Theatre KIDDSTUFF New Play Competition for her book and lyrics to *Pinocchio*. Her further credits include *That's Life, This Week in the Suburbs,* and *A Christmas Valentine.*

Judy Freed wrote the children's musical *Tickle Cakes,* which has toured three states and was recognized by the American Alliance for Theatre & Education. Her musical *Tantrum on the Tracks* was commissioned by the Duncan YMCA of Chicago. Adult musicals include *Emma & Company; Me and Al,* which was showcased at the International Festival of Musical Theatre in Cardiff, Wales; and *Sleepy Hollow,* which was developed at the ASCAP/Disney Musical Theater Workshop.

Jim Hughes is a Professor Emeritus at Oakland (CA) University's School of Education. He also worked on education projects in Kenya, Nepal, Indonesia, Yemen Arab Republic, and Pakistan. He is co-author of twenty-one texts in elementary social studies. He is also a published playwright in musical theatre, and his plays have been produced in regional theatres in New Mexico, California, and Colorado. Currently he is working on the books and lyrics for several musicals.

Carmen Tafolla has served as Director of the Mexican-American Studies Center at Texas Lutheran College, Assistant Professor of Women's Studies at California State University Fresno, and Special Assistant to the President for Cultural Diversity Programming at Northern Arizona University. She has published books of poetry, television screenplays, and numerous short stories. Her stories for children include *Baby Coyote and the Old Woman, Take a Bite,* and *The Dog Who Wanted to Be a Tiger.*

What Will I Be?

by Alisha Fran-Potter

A zebra wants to be like many animals. But he comes back home.

CHARACTERS

 SAM

 JEN

 ZEBRA

 HIPPO

 ELEPHANT

 BIRD

 PIG

 DUCK

 RAT

WORDS TO READ

air	want
be	why

1

ZEBRA Look at the birds.

They can play in the air.

They can come and go as they like.

 HIPPO Yes, I like to watch them.

I like the way they go up and up.

 ELEPHANT They look glad to be up in the air.

 ZEBRA I am a zebra. I like my home in this park.

But I want to be like many animals too.

I will go to be with them.

SCENE 2

 JEN Here I am, animals.

 SAM Here I am too.

 ELEPHANT AND HIPPO Here is Jen.

Here is Sam.

 JEN Do you want a snack?

 ELEPHANT AND HIPPO Yes!

SAM But where is the Zebra?

HIPPO He left the park. He went on a trip.

JEN Where did he go?

 ELEPHANT He went to see many animals.

 SAM Why did he go?

 HIPPO He wants to be like them.

 JEN We will miss him.

  ELEPHANT AND HIPPO We will too!

 SAM Will he come back?

SCENE 3

 BIRD Zebra, why are you here?

 ZEBRA Bird, I have come from the park.
I want to be with you. Help me act like a bird.

 BIRD Come be a bird.
Flap your legs like this.
You can go up in the air.
Flap, flap, flap.

 ZEBRA I will flap my legs. Flap, flap, flap.
But I can not go up in the air. It is too bad.
I can not be a bird. I will go see the Pig.

© Pearson Education 1

PIG Zebra, why are you here?

 ZEBRA Pig, I have come from the park.
I want to be with you. Help me act like a pig.

 PIG Come be a pig.
Jump in the mud like this.
Jump, jump, jump.

 ZEBRA I will jump in the mud. Jump, jump, jump.
But I do not like the mud.
I can not be a pig. I will go see the Duck.

 DUCK Zebra, why are you here?

 ZEBRA Duck, I have come from the park.
I want to be with you. Help me act like a duck.

 DUCK Come be a duck.
Swim in the pond like this.
Swim, swim, swim.
Go quack, quack, quack!

 ZEBRA I will go quack. Quack, quack, quack.
I can quack, but I can not swim in the pond.
It is too bad. I can not be a duck.
I will go see the Rat.

RAT Zebra, why are you here?

 ZEBRA Rat, I have come from the park.
I want to be with you. Help me act like a rat.

 RAT Come be a rat.
Run like this. Run, run, run.
Sniff like this. Sniff, sniff, sniff.

 ZEBRA I will run. Run, run, run.
I can run, but I can not sniff like you.
It is too bad. I can not be a rat.
I will be a Zebra and go on my way.
I will go back to the park.

SCENE 4

 ZEBRA Here I am.

 SAM Here is Zebra!

 ZEBRA Did you miss me?

 JEN Yes. Zebra, we are glad you are back.

 HIPPO Where did you go?

 ZEBRA I went to see many animals.

ELEPHANT What animals did you see?

 ZEBRA I saw Bird, Pig, Duck, and Rat.

 HIPPO What did you do?

 ZEBRA I did flap my legs like Bird.
But I did not go up in the air.
I did jump in the mud like Pig.
I did quack like Duck.
But I did not swim in the pond.
I did run like Rat.
But I did not sniff.

 SAM Was it fun?

 ZEBRA No. It was too bad for me.
I have come home.
I want to be with you. I like to be a Zebra.
I like my home in this park.

 JEN You can eat a snack.

 SAM You can play with the animals here.

 ZEBRA Yes, I like that!

Kate Goes to the Fun Fest

by Susan DiLallo

A Fun Fest is best when everybody
in the neighborhood helps out.

CHARACTERS

KATE (6 years)

LUKE, her brother (9 years)

MOM

DAD

MR. MACK, the milk man

MR. GREEN, the snack shop man

MRS. LEE, Kim's mom

MRS. DUTTON, Kate's teacher

KIM (7 years)

WORDS TO READ

about	today
day	very
happy	

LUKE Today is the day of the Fun Fest.
My sis, Kate, and I are going. My name is Luke.
Mom and Dad are going too. Kate is happy.
She is telling all the people we meet.

KATE Look, Luke, there is our milk man, Mr. Mack.
Good day, Mr. Mack.

MR. MACK Good day, Kate.
I see you have a big smile.
You must be glad about something.

KATE Oh, yes. Today is the Fun Fest.
I am very happy. We are going to go.

MR. MACK The Fun Fest!
I bet you will go on a lot of fun rides.

KATE Yes, I like to go on rides. Look, Luke.
There is the man who works in the snack shop.
Good day, Mr. Green.

MR. GREEN Good day, Kate.
My, what a big smile you have today.

KATE Yes. Today is the Fun Fest.
I am very happy. We are going to go.

MR. GREEN The Fun Fest!
I bet there will be a lot of good food to eat there.

KATE Yes, I will like to have something to eat there.
Look, Luke, that's Kim's mom. Hello, Mrs. Lee.

MRS. LEE Hello, Kate.
Are you all set for the big Fun Fest?

KATE Oh, yes, and I am very happy.

MRS. LEE Yes, Kim is too.
There will be lots of fun games to play.
When you get there, you will see her.

KATE Look, Luke, there's my teacher.
Good day, Mrs. Dutton.

MRS. DUTTON Good day, Kate.

KATE Mrs. Dutton, this is Luke.

MRS. DUTTON I'm glad to meet you, Luke.

LUKE Hello, Mrs. Dutton.

MRS. DUTTON Kate, why do you have that smile?
Is it for the Fun Fest?

KATE Yes. I did not go to the last Fun Fest.
I am very happy to go to this one.

MRS. DUTTON I'm glad you are happy.
And I bet you will win lots of fun prizes.

KATE Luke, do all the people in town go?
Do they all go to the Fun Fest?

LUKE Yes. The Fun Fest is very big in this town.
And all the people have fun at it.

SCENE 2

MOM There you are, Kate and Luke.
We are set to go to the Fun Fest. Are you?

KATE Yes, we are, Mom.

DAD Good. Let us get in the van.
We can go there now.

LUKE We ride in the van.
When we get to the town, we see lots of big tents.
The tents have green and yellow stripes on them.
And there are a hundred people walking around.

KATE Look! There's a hippo ride that will go up in the air.
Can I go on that?

MOM Yes, you can go.
And do you see the man who runs the ride?

KATE Why, Mr. Mack, what are you doing here?
You are the milk man.
What are you doing at the Fun Fest?

MR. MACK I run this ride. See?
I press the button that makes the hippos go.
They go up and down and around and around.
Do you want to ride?

KATE Oh, yes. I like to ride!

MR. MACK Well then, hop on.

KATE Come on, Luke.

LUKE Here I am. I will ride this yellow hippo.

KATE And I will ride this blue one.
Wheee . . . this is fun!

LUKE I like to ride the hippos.

MR. MACK See?
There are lots of fun rides here!

SCENE 3

KATE All those rides made me thirsty.
Can we get some food now, Dad?

DAD Yes. We will go into the food tent.

KATE Why, Mr. Green. What are you doing here?

MR. GREEN I am fixing the food in this tent.
I am making hot dogs and other good food.
Do you want a hot dog?

KATE Yes, I do. Can I have some milk too?

MR. GREEN Here you go. See? I told you.
I said there is good food here.

DAD We could play some games now, if you like.

MOM Good! They have games in that big tent.
We will go there now.

KATE Why, Mrs. Lee, what are you doing here?

MRS. LEE I run the games in this tent.
Do you want to play a game?

KATE Oh, yes.

MRS. LEE Here. Toss the bag.
Get the bag in a circle.
Just stand on the line and toss.

KATE This is fun!

MRS. LEE See?
There are lots of games to play.

LUKE Look, Kate. Your bag landed in the blue circle.
You win a prize!

MRS. LEE You can go to the prize tent.
You can pick out what prize you want.

KATE Wow! We will go there now.
Why, Mrs. Dutton! What are you doing here?

MRS. DUTTON I hand out prizes in this tent.
Take a look around, and tell me what you want.

SCENE 4

LUKE There are many dolls and other prizes.
Kate looks and looks. Then she picks one out.

KATE I like that big stuffed bear.
The yellow one on the top shelf.

MRS DUTTON Here it is.
You will take good care of it.

KIM Hello, Kate. I'm glad to see you.

KATE Hi, Kim. Your mom said to look for you here.

KIM I am glad you came. Isn't it fun?

KATE Yes! It is fun for you too?

KIM Yes. This is a good Fun Fest.
Did you just win that stuffed bear as a prize?

KATE Yes, I did. Did you win a prize too?

KIM Yes, I did. I got a Jack in the Box. See?

LUKE Soon it is time to go.
On the way home, we talk about what we did.
We talk about all the people we saw.

MOM Mr. Green made the food.

DAD Mr. Mack ran the Hippo Ride.

LUKE Kim's mom ran the games.

KATE And Mrs. Dutton gave out prizes.

MOM Yes. Many people in the neighborhood helped.
Why, if we did not have their help, then what?
There might not be a Fun Fest at all.

LUKE When I am big, I want to help out.
I will help at the Fun Fest.
I want to run the rides.

DAD Yes, that will be nice, Luke.

KATE And I will hand out prizes.

MOM I know you will be good at that, Kate.

KATE Yes. But now . . . I just want to hug my bear!

Flowers in January

by Judy Freed
based on a Czech folktale

You may get what you want
if you are nice and fun—
and if you have a good heart.

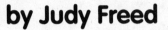

CHARACTERS

GRACE
PEG
MOTHER
JANUARY
FEBRUARY
MARCH
APRIL
MAY
JUNE
JULY
AUGUST
SEPTEMBER
OCTOBER
NOVEMBER
DECEMBER
STORYTELLERS 1–5
CHILDREN 1–3

WORDS TO READ

blow	month
full	snow
heart	

STORYTELLER 1 Long ago there was a girl called Grace. She was from a small town.

CHILD 1 I like Grace. She is always nice.

CHILD 2 I like Grace. She is always fun.

CHILD 3 I like Grace. She always works hard.

CHILD 1 Grace has a good heart.

STORYTELLER 2 Grace had no mother or father. She lived with a girl called Peg and with Peg's mother.

CHILD 1 I do not like Peg. She is not nice.

CHILD 2 I do not like Peg. She is not fun.

CHILD 3 I do not like Peg. She does not work hard.

CHILD 2 Peg does not have a good heart.

PEG Mother, I am so sad.

MOTHER Why are you sad, Peg?

PEG Everyone likes Grace more than they like me!

MOTHER Then we need to get rid of Grace.

STORYTELLER 3 Peg and her mother made up a plan.

PEG Grace!

GRACE Yes, Peg.

PEG I want some flowers. Go to the forest. Find me some flowers.

GRACE Peg, it is January. There are no flowers in January.

MOTHER Grace. You live in our house. You eat our food. You must do what we tell you. See?

GRACE Yes.

MOTHER Now go to the forest. Find Peg some flowers. Do not come back until you find them.

STORYTELLER 4 So Grace got her scarf and left the house.

PEG She will not find flowers. She will not come back!

SCENE 2

STORYTELLER 5 The forest was full of snow and ice. Grace could not find flowers anywhere.

GRACE What will I do? I cannot go home if I have no flowers!

STORYTELLER 1 Grace got very cold. Then she saw some people sitting by a fire.

GRACE Could you help me, please?

DECEMBER What do you want?

GRACE I want to warm my hands by your fire.

NOVEMBER Come and sit down.

OCTOBER Why are you out in the snow and the ice?

GRACE I have to find flowers.

SEPTEMBER There are no flowers in January!

GRACE I know. But if I don't find flowers, I can not go home again.

AUGUST That is very sad.

JULY What's your name?

GRACE Grace. What's yours?

JUNE We are the 12 months.

JANUARY January brings ice and snow.

FEBRUARY In February cold winds blow.

MARCH In March some flowers can be seen. I am the month of March. I can grow you flowers.

STORYTELLER 2 March clapped its hands. Flowers grew at her feet.

GRACE Thank you so much!

MARCH Take all the flowers you need.

STORYTELLER 3 Grace picked some and went back to her house.

PEG Why are you here? I wanted you to get flowers.

GRACE I have flowers. See?

MOTHER There are no flowers in January.

GRACE But I have them. Here, Peg.

STORYTELLER 4 Peg tossed the flowers down.

PEG I hate flowers! I want grapes.

GRACE Grapes?

PEG Go to the forest. Find me some grapes.

GRACE Peg, it is January. There are no grapes in January.

MOTHER Grace. You live in our house. You eat our food. You must do what we tell you. See?

GRACE Yes.

MOTHER Now go to the forest. Find Peg some grapes. Do not come back until you find them.

STORYTELLER 5 So Grace picked up the flowers and left the house.

PEG She will not find grapes. She will not come back!

SCENE 3

STORYTELLER 1 The forest was full of snow and ice. Grace saw the 12 months sitting by the fire.

GRACE Here are your flowers. They are very beautiful.

MARCH Why don't you keep them?

GRACE Now I have to find grapes.

APRIL There are no grapes in January.

JANUARY January brings ice and snow.

FEBRUARY In February cold winds blow.

MARCH In March some flowers can be seen.

APRIL By April grass and trees are green.

MAY In May the air is warm and sweet.

JUNE June brings fresh food for all to eat.

JULY July brings carrots, corn, and peas.

AUGUST In August there are more of these.

SEPTEMBER September brings grapes for one and all.
I am September. If you need grapes, I can get
you grapes.

STORYTELLER 2 September clapped its hands. Grapes fell
at her feet.

GRACE Thank you so much!

SEPTEMBER Those grapes are all I can get.

STORYTELLER 3 Grace went back to her house.

GRACE Here are your grapes.

STORYTELLER 4 By then Peg and her mother were very
hungry. They ate the grapes in no time.

MOTHER Where did you get those grapes?

GRACE September gave them to me. I met the
12 months in the forest.

PEG I want more grapes! Get me more grapes!

GRACE I can not. September has no more grapes
to give.

MOTHER Then Peg and I will get more grapes. Grace,
you stay here.

SCENE 4

STORYTELLER 5 Peg and her mother went to the forest.
The forest was full of snow and ice. They saw the
12 months sitting around the fire. Peg started to yell.

PEG I want grapes! Get me grapes!

NOVEMBER Oh, do not yell. It hurts my ears.

STORYTELLER 1 Peg started to kick.

PEG I want grapes! Get me grapes!

MAY Oh, do not kick. It hurts my legs.

STORYTELLER 2 Peg started to toss things.

PEG I want grapes! Get me grapes!

OCTOBER Do not toss things.

MOTHER If you want her to stop, then give her what
she wants.

DECEMBER But it is January. There are no grapes in
January.

JANUARY January brings snow and ice.

FEBRUARY You have not been very nice.

MARCH In March some flowers can be seen.

APRIL You have been so bad and mean!

MAY In May the air is warm and sweet.

JUNE You will not get more grapes to eat.

JULY July brings many types of food.

AUGUST The way you ask is very rude!

SEPTEMBER I have grapes, yes I do.

OCTOBER But September will not give them to you.

NOVEMBER We will bring you ice and snow.

DECEMBER We will bring you winds that blow.

12 MONTHS (all together) Now go!

STORYTELLER 3 And with that, a huge wind came up. When the wind stopped, Peg and her mother were gone.

CHILD 3 Then Grace had a party for all her friends. The 12 months were there too.

CHILD 1 Everyone ate grapes. They looked at the beautiful flowers.

CHILD 2 And no one missed Peg or her mother at all.

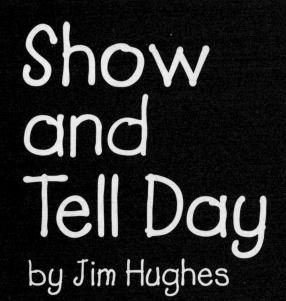

Show and Tell Day

by Jim Hughes

Gina wants to bring a surprise for Show and Tell Day. What she brings is a treasure.

CHARACTERS

STORYTELLER
GINA
MOM
MRS. LOTT
TOMÁS
KEN
GILBERT
NAN
MAY
MR. BLACK
CHILDREN
YOYO, the dog

WORDS TO READ

India
Indonesia   New Mexico
Kenya   Tanzania
Nepal   Uganda

STORYTELLER Gina is in first grade. She likes school. Yet, now she is sad.

GINA I don't want to go to school.

MOM Why not?

GINA It is my turn for Show and Tell Day. I have nothing to show.

MOM What about one of your dolls?

GINA Many children will bring dolls. Mrs. Lott said to bring things that we treasure. I do not want to bring a doll. I want to bring a surprise.

MOM What about the stamp from Kenya? It is on your letter from Rich.

GINA It is too small. No one will see it.

MOM What about your zebra? It came from Tanzania.

GINA Yes. But Gilbert is bringing an elephant. It is made from the leaves of a tree. It is very big. It is much nicer than my zebra. I want a real treasure.

MOM I have a plan. It is Show and Tell Day.

GINA Yes, Mom.

MOM Some children will show, and some children will tell?

© Pearson Education 1

GINA Yes, Mom. But I have nothing to show. I have nothing to tell.

MOM I will help you. Can you bring a pet to school?

GINA I can if Mrs. Lott tells me yes.

MOM I will call her. If she tells me yes, I will bring Yoyo to your class.

YOYO Yip, yip, yip!

GINA Yes, Mom, yes! Yoyo is a treasure! I will be glad to show her and tell about her.

SCENE 2

STORYTELLER Gina went to school. She was very glad. Children had many things for Show and Tell.

MRS. LOTT Gilbert, would you show us your animal?

GILBERT This is an elephant. It is made from banana leaves.

MRS. LOTT How did you get it?

GILBERT My father came from Uganda. He made it when he was a boy. Now, it is mine.

STORYTELLER On the map, Mrs. Lott showed the children where Uganda is.

MRS. LOTT Your father made the elephant. That is a treasure! Be very careful with it. It is May's turn now.

MAY This is my mom's necklace. It comes from Bombay, India. It is made from beads.

STORYTELLER On the map, Mrs. Lott showed the children where India is.

MRS. LOTT It is very beautiful. Your necklace is a treasure too.

STORYTELLER The children took turns. However, Gina sat still.

MRS. LOTT Nan, do you want to be next?

NAN Yes, Mrs. Lott. This is a shadow puppet. It comes from Indonesia.

STORYTELLER On the map, Mrs. Lott showed the children where Indonesia is.

MRS. LOTT Show us how it works. Look, children! Look at the shadow on the wall. That puppet is fun!

STORYTELLER Many children got up to show and tell. Mrs. Lott said Gina's mom was bringing a surprise. But she hadn't gotten there yet.

MRS. LOTT Tomás, do you have something to show?

TOMÁS Yes. It is a pot. It is made of clay. My grandmother made it for me.

MRS. LOTT Look, but don't touch, children. Where does the pot come from, Tomás?

TOMÁS My grandmother lives in the Acoma Pueblo (uh KOH muh PWEB loh) in New Mexico. It is on a high hill with a flat top.

STORYTELLER On the map, Mrs. Lott showed the children where New Mexico is.

SCENE 3

STORYTELLER Then Mr. Black came in to the classroom. Gina's mom was with him.

MR. BLACK Mrs. Lott, this is Gina's mom. She has a surprise for your children.

MRS. LOTT Thank you, Mr. Black. Gina, it is your turn now. What is your surprise?

STORYTELLER Gina's mom handed Gina a small dog. It was on a leash.

GINA This is my pet. Her name is Yoyo. She is a Lhasa apso (LAH suh AP soh) dog from Nepal. They are watch dogs.

STORYTELLER The children laughed. Yoyo was so small.

GILBERT How can that little dog be a watch dog?

GINA They bark if people come close.

MRS. LOTT They help you stay safe. When the dog barks, you know strange people are close.

MAY Can your dog do tricks?

GINA Yes. Yoyo can do many tricks.

STORYTELLER The children sat in a circle around Gina and Yoyo.

GINA First, she will sit for us. Sit, Yoyo.

STORYTELLER Some children were surprised when the dog sat.

KEN My dog can do that too.

GINA Can your dog do this? Get the ball, Yoyo!

STORYTELLER The little dog got the ball three times. Everyone laughed. Then Gina gave Yoyo a dog treat.

GINA Good dog, Yoyo! Good dog!

STORYTELLER The children all clapped. The dog barked.

YOYO Yip, yip, yip!

GINA If you are not afraid of Yoyo, she will shake hands with you.

KEN I will shake her hand.

STORYTELLER Ken put his hand slowly towards Yoyo. Then the dog lifted its paw, and Ken took it. Gina gave Yoyo more treats.

GINA Good Yoyo! Good dog!

YOYO Yip, yip, yip!

NAN Let me! Let me be next! I am not afraid of Yoyo.

STORYTELLER Nan took the dog's paw. Again, the children clapped.

NAN Let me give Yoyo a treat. Please!

GINA Be nice, Yoyo.

MRS. LOTT Yoyo is a nice dog. Yoyo is Gina's dog. But do we try to pet dogs we do not know?

ALL CHILDREN No! No! No!

GINA If you have a pet, you must take care of it.

MRS. LOTT How do you take care of Yoyo?

GINA Yoyo has to get shots from a vet. Yoyo has to have a tag, with a number.

GILBERT Like a car?

GINA Yes. See—here is Yoyo's tag.

STORYTELLER Gina showed the children the tag that Yoyo wore. She showed them all the numbers on the tag.

MRS. LOTT If Yoyo gets lost, the tag can help. The tag gives Gina's name.

KEN Lost dogs sometimes go to the Animal Shelter.

MRS. LOTT Very good, Ken. What other things do you do for Yoyo, Gina?

GINA I feed her every day. I make sure she has water in her dish.

TOMÁS Where does Yoyo sleep?

GINA Some dogs have a dog house. But Yoyo sleeps on my bed with me.

STORYTELLER The children laughed. Then those children that wanted to shake hands with Yoyo did.

YOYO Yip, yip, yip!

MRS. LOTT Well, Gina, you did bring a real treasure for Show and Tell!

STORYTELLER Then it was time for Gina, her mom, and Yoyo to go home.

YOYO Yip, yip, yip!

Do You Live in a Nest?

by Carmen Tafolla
adapted by Don Abramson

The animals in the forest are going to have a visitor. But where will she stay?

CHARACTERS

NARRATORS 1–2
CATERPILLARS 1–2
FROGS 1–2
TURTLES 1–2
DOGS 1–2
HORSES 1–2
BEARS 1–2
SQUIRRELS 1–2
BIRDS 1–2

NARRATOR 1 All the animals in the forest are happy.

NARRATOR 2 They have gotten some good news.

CATERPILLAR 1 Frog! Frog!

FROG 1 Hi, Caterpillar!

CATERPILLAR 2 I have good news!

FROG 2 Well, what is it?

CATERPILLAR 1 Bird is coming to visit.

FROG 1 I'm glad. Bird has a beautiful voice.

FROG 2 She makes the sweetest sounds.

CATERPILLAR 2 Where will she stay?

FROG 1 She can stay with me!

CATERPILLAR 1 Do you live in a nest?

FROG 2 No, I live in a nice, wet pond. There are lots of flies to eat.

FROG 1 Once Bird is here, she can pick which fly she wants.

CATERPILLAR 2 I don't think Bird wants a pond.

CATERPILLAR 1 She needs some place warmer than that.

TURTLE 1 Hi, Caterpillar! Hi, Frog!

FROG 2 Turtle! Turtle! Bird is coming to visit!

TURTLE 2 I'm glad. Bird has a beautiful voice.

TURTLE 1 I enjoy her music.

FROG 1 Where will she stay?

TURTLE 2 She can stay with me!

FROG 2 Do you live in a nest?

TURTLE 1 No, I live in a flat meadow by the pond. It has nice, green grass!

TURTLE 2 Once Bird is here, she can eat all the grass she wants.

FROG 1 I don't think Bird wants a meadow.

FROG 2 She needs some place rounder than that.

CATERPILLAR 2 She needs some place warmer.

DOG 1 Hi, Caterpillar! Hi, Frog! Hi, Turtle!

TURTLE 1 Dog! Dog! Bird is coming to visit!

DOG 2 I'm glad. Bird has a beautiful voice.

DOG 1 She makes the sweetest sounds.

TURTLE 2 Where will she stay?

DOG 2 She can stay with me!

TURTLE 1 Do you live in a nest?

DOG 1 No, I sleep on the ground under a big tree. There are lots of bones hidden under the tree!

DOG 2 Once Bird is here, she can pick which bone she wants.

TURTLE 2 I don't think Bird wants to sleep on the ground.

TURTLE 1 She needs some place higher than that.

FROG 1 She needs some place rounder.

CATERPILLAR 1 She needs some place warmer.

HORSE 1 Hi, Caterpillar! Hi, Frog!

HORSE 2 Hi, Turtle! Hi, Dog!

DOG 1 Horse! Horse! Bird is coming to visit!

HORSE 1 I'm glad. Bird has a beautiful voice.

HORSE 2 I enjoy her music.

DOG 2 Where will she stay?

HORSE 1 She can stay with me!

DOG 1 Do you live in a nest?

HORSE 2 No, I live in a nice big barn. There are many bundles of hay!

HORSE 1 Once Bird is here, she can pick any bundle she wants.

DOG 2 I don't think Bird wants a barn.

DOG 1 She needs some place smaller than that.

TURTLE 2 She needs some place higher.

FROG 2 She needs some place rounder.

CATERPILLAR 2 She needs some place warmer.

BEAR 1 Growl! Growl!

HORSE 2 Bear! Bear! Bird is coming to visit.

BEAR 2 I'm glad. Bird has a beautiful voice.

BEAR 1 She makes the sweetest sounds.

HORSE 1 Where will she stay?

BEAR 2 I do not like other animals in my way, but Bird is a visitor. She can stay with me!

HORSE 2 Do you live in a nest?

BEAR 1 No, I live in a cave under a great big rock. It is by the pond.

BEAR 2 There are lots of fish in the pond. Once Bird is here, she can pick which fish she wants.

HORSE 1 I don't think Bird wants a cave. She needs some place softer than that.

BEAR 1 You're right. Bird needs some place softer.

DOG 2 She needs some place smaller.

TURTLE 1 She needs some place higher.

FROG 1 She needs some place rounder.

CATERPILLAR 1 She needs some place warmer.

ALL Bird needs a nest!

NARRATOR 1 All the animals have a puzzle.

NARRATOR 2 Bird is coming to visit. Where will she stay?

NARRATOR 1 Who can solve the puzzle?

SQUIRREL 1 Hi, friends!

BEAR 2 Squirrel! Squirrel! Bird is coming to visit.

SQUIRREL 2 I'm glad. Bird has a beautiful voice.

SQUIRREL 1 I enjoy her music.

BEAR 1 She needs a place to stay.

BEAR 2 She needs a nest. But we do not live in nests.

BEAR 1 Do you live in a nest?

SQUIRREL 2 Yes, but my kind of nest is not the kind of nest that Bird needs.

BEAR 2 Then what will we do?

SQUIRREL 1 I know. I have an idea.

SQUIRREL 2 I can solve the puzzle.

BEAR 1 How?

SQUIRREL 1 We will make a new nest for Bird. It will be just right for her.

ALL Yes! That is a great idea!

SQUIRREL 2 Horse, get us some hay from the barn.

HORSE 2 Here it is.

SQUIRREL 1 Thank you for the hay, Horse. Now, Dog, you can make it round.

DOG 1 I know how to do that.

DOG 2 I know about round things.

DOG 1 I love to play with a ball.

SQUIRREL 2 Turtle, you can press a warm place in the hay for Bird.

TURTLE 2 I know how to do that.

SQUIRREL 1 There. It's ready.

CATERPILLAR 2 Thank you, Squirrel. It is a great nest.

FROG 2 Where do we put it?

HORSE 1 I know where we can find the tallest tree!

CATERPILLAR 1 How do we get it up in the tree?

SQUIRREL 2 Bear, pick it up and put it on my back. I will jump up into the tree.

SQUIRREL 1 I will put Bird's nest high up in the leaves.

SCENE 3

NARRATOR 2 All the animals in the forest are happy.

NARRATOR 1 Bird is coming to visit, and they have a new nest for her to stay in.

BIRD 1 Caterpillar! Caterpillar! I've come to visit!

CATERPILLAR 2 Hi, Bird. I'm glad to see you.

BIRD 1 I have a friend with me. I hope you don't mind.

FROG 1 Not at all. It's good to meet you.

BIRD 2 Hi, everyone.

TURTLE 1 We have a nest for you! Do you like it?

BIRD 1 Oh, it's the softest, smallest, highest, roundest, warmest nest of all!

BIRD 2 Which one of you made the nest?

DOG 2 We all helped each other.

BIRD 1 Well, thank you. You are all good friends.

HORSE 2 Now we can help each other do one more thing.

ALL Yes! Let's have a party!

Poetry Interpretation

When you **interpret** a poem, you read it out loud. Other people listen while you read. They are your **audience.** You can use your *voice,* your *body,* and your *face* as you read. You can help your audience understand the poem.

USE YOUR VOICE

First read the poem to yourself. Be sure you understand every word. Also be sure you know how to say every word. If you are not sure about a word, ask your teacher or look in a dictionary.

When you read a poem aloud, it should sound like the way people talk. Look for sentences. Look for a period, an exclamation mark, or a question mark. You don't have to stop at every rhyme. You don't have to stop at the end of every line.

Listen for rhythm When you **emphasize** a word or syllable, you say it strongly. It makes a beat. Sometimes a poem has a strong beat, or **rhythm.** It's easy and fun to read a poem like that. Look at this poem:

> A wise old owl lived in an oak;
> The more he saw the less he spoke;
> The less he spoke the more he heard.
> Why can't we all be like that wise old bird?

Because of its strong rhythm, you might read the second line like this:

> the MORE he SAW the LESS he SPOKE

In most lines, the beat or rhythm is on every other word. It doesn't matter if the word is big or small. But not every line of poetry has the same kind of rhythm.

Group words in phrases You can also group words. A grouping is a **phrase.** A phrase should make sense and help your audience understand. If you group words and you emphasize the important words, the first line of the poem might sound like this:

> a WISE OLD OWL   LIVED   in an OAK

Say the line by grouping the words. Do you hear the difference when you group words?

What do the other lines sound like when you group words and emphasize important words?

Speak loudly enough Speaking loudly does not mean shouting. Use your normal voice, but speak so that the people in the back row of seats can hear you.

Make it sound interesting Use your voice to make your audience want to listen to you. Here are some things you can do:

- People can tell from the way your voice sounds if you are happy, fearful, excited, or angry.

- Let your voice go up and down when that feels right.

- Use different speeds. Some poems sound best when they are read quickly. Other poems sound best when they are read slowly.

- You can also use a **pause**—take a short break between words or phrases.

USE YOUR BODY

Stand up straight and tall. Your voice comes out better when you do. You can hold your paper in one hand and make movements with your other hand. Don't make too many movements. That keeps the audience from listening to your words. Use your movements to give your poem meaning.

USE YOUR FACE

Your face also shows if you are happy or sad. Show a happy face for a happy poem. Show a sad face for a sad poem. Sometimes you need to change your face for different lines in the same poem.

ACT A CHARACTER

Who is the speaker in the poem? A boy or girl? An animal? A tree or flower? If you can tell who the speaker is, you can act like that character. First imagine that you are the character. Then use the voice that character would use. Use movements of your face, body, and hands the way the character would.

PERFORM FOR AN AUDIENCE

Here are some things you can do when you read a poem for others:

Practice your reading Don't just practice once. Practice several times. If you know your poem very well, you can perform it better.

Take your time When you step in front of your audience, pause. Take a deep breath. Think about what you are doing. Then start. At the end, take your time again. Look at your audience. Smile to let them know you are finished.

Look at your audience You can't read and look at your audience at the same time. But if you know the poem well, you can look at your audience now and then. That will help keep their attention.

When you make a mistake If you say a word wrong, just go back and read the whole sentence again. If you lose your place, stop long enough to find it. Don't say, "No, wait" or "Excuse me." Just think about what you did wrong and then do it right.

Choral Reading

The name **choral reading** means reading aloud in a group, like a chorus or choir. Sometimes the readers take turns, and sometimes they speak all together. It can be fun to read a poem together.

Practice effectively To give a good choral performance, you must practice. This is not a time to call attention to yourself. This is a time to blend into the group.

Follow directions The teacher or director will tell you when to start reading by yourself or all together. Listen carefully when other people read. Follow on your paper. Keep your place so you can come in when it is your turn.

Pay attention Even if you are not reading, you are still on stage. You are part of the big picture. You need to help the audience pay attention too.

Enter and exit smoothly You should also practice how you will come in, where you will stand, and how you will leave. You want to make your entrance and exit quick and smooth.

Unit 1 Animals, Tame and Wild

Puppy
by Lee Bennett Hopkins

We bought our puppy
    A brand new bed
But he likes sleeping
    On mine instead.
I'm glad he does
    'Cause I'd miss his cold nose
Waking me up,
    Tickling my toes.

Unit 1 Animals, Tame and Wild

Kittens
by Myra Cohn Livingston

Our cat had kittens
weeks ago
when everything outside was snow.

So she stayed in
and kept them warm
and safe from all the clouds and storm.

But yesterday
when there was sun
she snuzzled on the smallest one

and turned it over
from beneath
and took its fur between her teeth

and carried it
outside to see
how nice a winter day can be

and then our dog
decided he
would help her take the other three

and one by one
they took them out
to see what sun is all about

so when they're grown
they'll always know
to never be afraid of snow.

Making Friends

by Eloise Greenfield

when I was in kindergarten
this new girl came in our class one day
and the teacher told her to sit beside me
and I didn't know what to say
so I wiggled my nose and made my
bunny face
and she laughed
then she puffed out her cheeks
and she made a funny face
and I laughed
so then
we were friends

Unit 3 Changes

The End
by A. A. Milne

When I was One,
I had just begun.

When I was Two,
I was nearly new.

When I was Three,
I was hardly Me.

When I was Four,
I was not much more.

When I was Five,
I was just alive.

But now I am Six,
   I'm clever as clever.
So I think I'll be six now
   for ever and ever.

Everything Grows
by Raffi

A blade of grass, fingers and toes,
Hair on my head, a red, red rose.
Everything grows, anyone knows,
That's how it goes.

Everything grows and grows.
Babies do, animals too.
Everything grows.
Everything grows and grows.
Sisters do, brothers too.
Everything grows.

Food on the farm, fish in the sea,
Birds in the air, leaves on the tree.
Everything grows, anyone knows,
That's how it goes.

Everything grows and grows.
Babies do, animals too.
Everything grows.
Everything grows and grows.
Sisters do, brothers too.
Everything grows.

That's how it goes, under the sun.
That's how it goes, under the rain.
Everything grows, anyone knows,
That's how it goes.

Everything grows and grows.
Babies do, animals too.
Everything grows.
Everything grows and grows.
Sisters do, brothers too.
Everything grows.

Unit 4 Treasures

Honey Bear
by Elizabeth Lang

There was a big bear
Who lived in a cave;
His greatest love
Was honey.
He had twopence a week
Which he could never save,
So he never had
Any money.
I bought him a money box
Red and round,
in which to put
his money.
He saved and saved
Till he got a pound,
Then spent it all
On honey.

---

twopence two pennies
pound a unit of money in England, like the U. S. dollar

Sunflakes
by Frank Asch

If sunlight fell like snowflakes,
gleaming yellow and so bright,
we could build a sunman,
we could have a sunball fight,
we could watch the sunflakes
drifting in the sky.
We could go sleighing
in the middle of July
through sundrifts and sunbanks,
we could ride a sunmobile,
and we could touch sunflakes—
I wonder how they'd feel.

Unit 5 Great Ideas

Quack, Quack!
by Dr. Seuss

We have two ducks. One blue. One black.
And when our blue duck goes "Quack-quack"
our black duck quickly quack-quacks back.
The quacks Blue quacks make her quite a quacker
but Black is a quicker quacker-backer.

I Speak, I Say, I Talk
by Arnold L. Shapiro

Cats purr.

Lions roar.

Owls hoot.

Bears snore.

Crickets creak.

Mice squeak.

Sheep baa.

But I SPEAK!

Monkeys chatter.

Cows moo.

Ducks quack.

Doves coo.

Pigs squeal.

Horses neigh.

Chickens cluck.

But I SAY!

Flies hum.

Dogs growl.

Bats screech.

Coyotes howl.

Frogs croak.

Parrots squawk.

Bees buzz.

But I TALK!